National Parks

Rocky Mountain National Park

M.C. Hall

Heinemann Library
Chicago, Illinois

© 2006 Heinemann Library
a division of Reed Elsevier Inc.
Chicago, Illinois

Customer Service 888-454-2279
Visit our website at www.heinemannlibrary.com

Page layout by Richard Parker and Maverick Design
Photo research by Maria Joannou
Illustrations by Jeff Edwards
Printed and bound in China by South China Printing Company Limited

10 09 08 07 06
10 9 8 7 6 5 4 3 2 1

Library of Congress Cataloging-in-Publication Data
Hall, Margaret, 1947-
    Rocky Mountain National Park / Margaret Hall.
        p. cm. -- (National parks)
Includes bibliographical references and index.
ISBN 1-4034-6701-3 (lib. bdg.) -- ISBN 1-4034-6708-0 (pbk.)
1. Rocky Mountain National Park (Colo.)--Juvenile literature. I. Title.
    F782.R59H35 2005
    978.8'69--dc22
                            2004030390

Acknowledgments
The author and publishers are grateful to the following for permission to reproduce copyright material:
Alamy pp. 5 (Andre Jenny), 25 (David Boag), 12 (Gareth McCormack), 10 (Ginny Santora), 11 (James Frank), 16 (Robert E. Barber); Corbis pp. 29, 30, 31, 32, Corbis 20 (Andrew Brown), 22 (Buddy Mays), 7 (Conrad Zobel), 24 (W. Perry Conway); Denver Public Library p. 8 (Western History/Genealogy Department); Getty Images/ Imagebank pp. 23 (Art Wolfe), 13 (Tyler Stableford); Getty Images/Stone p. 4 (Bob Thomason); Inmagine/Photodisc p. 17; Library of Congress p. 9; Lonely Planet Images pp. 26 (John Elk III), 21 (Richard Cummins); National Park Service pp. 14, 15, 18, 27; Terragalleria p. 19

Cover photograph of Rocky Mountains reproduced with permission of Lonely Planet Images

Some words are shown in bold, **like this**. You can find out what they mean by looking in the glossary.

Contents

Our National Parks 4

Rocky Mountain National Park 6

Rocky Mountain National Park
    Long Ago 8

Visiting Rocky Mountain National Park . 10

The Mountains 12

Exploring the Mountains 14

Lakes, Streams, and Waterfalls 16

Park Plants 18

Above the Timberline 20

Park Animals 22

More Animals 24

Park Buildings and People 26

Map of Rocky Mountain National Park . 28

Timeline 29

Glossary 30

Find Out More 31

Index 32

Our National Parks

National parks are areas of land set aside for people to visit and enjoy **nature**. These parks do not belong to one person. They belong to everyone in the United States.

There are more than 50 national parks in the United States. Rocky Mountain National Park is visited by around three million people each year.

Rocky Mountain National Park

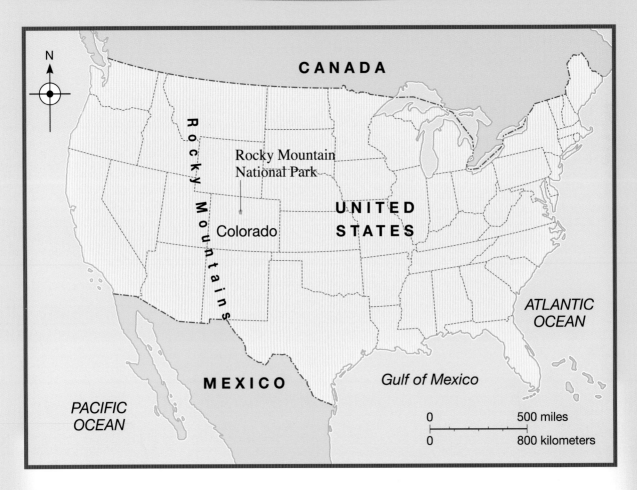

N

CANADA

Rocky Mountains

Rocky Mountain
National Park

Colorado

UNITED
STATES

MEXICO

Gulf of Mexico

PACIFIC
OCEAN

ATLANTIC
OCEAN

0   500 miles

0   800 kilometers

Rocky Mountain National Park is in the
western part of the United States. The park
is located in the state of Colorado.

The park is named for the Rocky Mountains. This **mountain range** runs through the entire park.

Rocky Mountain National Park Long Ago

Native Americans were the first people to live in the area that is now Rocky Mountain National Park. Later, white men came to trap animals for their fur.

Bert Gross trapped animals in the park from 1890.

Early visitors to Rocky Mountain National Park came on horseback.

In the late 1800s, small towns grew up near the mountains. In 1915 the United States **government** set aside land to become Rocky Mountain National Park.

Visiting Rocky Mountain National Park

Most people visit Rocky Mountain National Park in the spring, summer, and fall. They come to hike, camp, fish, and see **wildlife**.

Winters are very snowy. However, some parts of the park stay open. People come to **snowshoe** and cross-country ski on park trails.

The Mountains

Rocky Mountain National Park has some of the highest mountains in the United States. Longs Peak is the tallest mountain in the park.

Longs Peak

Park visitors can hike on trails in the mountains. Mountain climbers can climb to the top of some of the mountains.

Exploring the Mountains

Trail Ridge Road

Park visitors can also drive through the mountains. Trail Ridge Road is open from late May to fall. It is the highest **paved** road in the United States.

A **gondola** goes to the top of one mountain. People can ride it to get views of the mountains. In the winter, the gondola carries skiers to the top.

Lakes, Streams, and Waterfalls

There are many beautiful lakes in Rocky Mountain National Park. Some lakes are high in the mountains. Others are in **valleys** between the mountains.

Nymph Lake

The park also has many rocky streams. In some places, the land suddenly drops downhill. The water from the streams forms waterfalls.

Park Plants

Much of Rocky Mountain National Park is covered with forests. There are many **evergreens** and aspen trees.

There are also **meadows** filled with grass and wildflowers like Indian paintbrush and bear grass. These meadows are found in the **valleys**.

Above the Timberline

Many parts of the park are above the **timberline**. That means that the weather is too cold and windy for trees to grow.

Only small plants can grow above the timberline. There are twisted bushes and wildflowers. Rocks are covered with tiny plants called **lichen**.

lichen

Park Animals

Some large animals like mountain lions live in the mountains. Visitors may also see bighorn sheep climbing up the steep slopes.

Male bighorn sheep have large horns.

elk

Other large animals live in the **valleys** of the park. Visitors may see moose near lakes and streams. They may also see **herds** of elk.

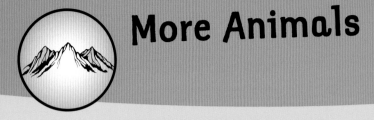

More Animals

yellow bellied marmot

Rocky Mountain National Park is also home to many small animals. Eagles live high in the mountains. So do small furry animals called the marmot and the pika.

Otters and beavers live near streams and lakes. Deer, mice, chipmunks, and other animals live in the forests and **meadows** of the park.

least chipmunk

Park Buildings and People

Rocky Mountain National Park has five visitor centers. People stop at the centers to get information about the park. There is also a museum that tells about the history of the area.

Park rangers work at the visitor centers and in other places around the park. The rangers lead hikes, give talks, and teach people about the mountains and the **wildlife**.

Map of Rocky Mountain National Park

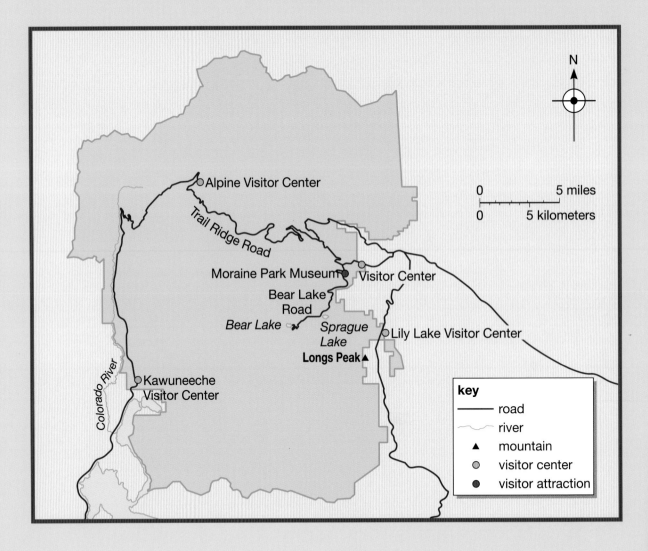

Alpine Visitor Center

Trail Ridge Road

Moraine Park Museum • Visitor Center

Bear Lake Road

Bear Lake

Sprague Lake

Longs Peak ▲

○ Lily Lake Visitor Center

Colorado River

○ Kawuneeche Visitor Center

N

| 0 | | | | | | 5 miles |
| 0 | | | | | | 5 kilometers |

key
— road
〰 river
▲ mountain
⬤ visitor center
⬤ visitor attraction

Timeline

11,000 years ago	Native Americans use trails through the mountains
late 1700s	Trappers come for beaver and other animals
1820s	Major Stephen Long maps area near the park. Longs Peak will be named for him.
1859	First white settlers move to area near park
1868	John Wesley Powell is the first to climb Longs Peak
1876	Colorado becomes a state
1915	United States **government** establishes Rocky Mountain National Park
1932	Trail Ridge Road opens
1990	The park expands by adding the area around Lily Lake
1993	"Hotshots" firefighters make the park their home base

Glossary

evergreen tree that does not lose its leaves in the winter. Most evergreens have needlelike leaves.

gondola enclosed car that hangs from a cable and is used to take people up and down a mountain

government group of people that makes laws for and runs a country

herd large group of animals such as elk or deer

lichen tiny plants that grow on rocks

meadow large grassy field

mountain range long row of mountains

national park natural area set aside by the government for people to visit

nature the outdoors and the wild plants and animals found there

park ranger man or woman who works in a national park and shares information about the wildlife and unusual sights of the park

paved covered with a hard surface

snowshoe to travel on top of the snow on snowshoes that are attached to boots

timberline point above which trees cannot grow

valley low area between hills or mountains

wildlife wild animals of an area

Find Out More

Books

An older reader can help you with these books:

Domeniconi, David. *M Is for Majestic: A National Parks Alphabet.* Farmington Hills, Mich.: Gale Group, 2003.

Gilda, Robert. *Bighorn Sheep: Mountain Monarchs.* Minneapolis, Minn.: Econo-Clad Books, 2001.

Graf, Mike. *Rocky Mountain National Park.* Mankato, Minn.: Bridgestone, 2002.

Mader, Jan. *Rocky Mountains.* San Francisco, Calif.: Children's Press, 2004.

Raatma, Lucia. *Our National Parks.* Mankato, Minn.: Compass Point Books, 2002.

Stone, Lynn. *America's National Parks.* Vero Beach, Fla.: Rourke Publishing, 2002.

Address

To find out more about Rocky Mountain National Park, write to:

Rocky Mountain National Park
1000 Highway 36
Estes Park, CO 80517

Index

animals 10, 22–25

climbing 13

fur trappers 8, 29

gondola 15

hiking 10, 13, 27

lakes and streams 16, 17, 23, 29
lichen 21
location 6
Longs Peak 12, 29

maps 6, 28
meadows 19, 25
mountains 7, 12, 14, 15, 16, 24

national parks 4–5, 9, 29
Native Americans 8, 29

rangers 27

skiing 11, 15

timberline 20
Trail Ridge Road 14, 29
trails 13
trees and plants 18–21

valleys 16, 19
visitor centers 26

waterfalls 17
weather 11, 20
winter 11, 15